Module 1: Academic Cultu

Introduction

The transition between secondary and higher education can be a time of upheaval. You will need to learn about the customs and expectations of your new college or university. In addition, you will need to work alongside other students and academics from a wide range of backgrounds. This module will help you to understand the academic culture that exists in higher education in the UK, as well as touching on cross-cultural communication.

Unit 1 defines academic culture and checks understanding of key concepts. Unit 2 facilitates discussion of common problems associated with the transition to higher education. Unit 3 attempts to challenge any unrealistic expectations you may have about higher education. Unit 4 examines common communication problems and will help you to avoid cross-cultural misunderstandings in an academic environment. Unit 5 focuses on time management, which is an important value in British culture, and it will help you use your time more efficiently. Finally, Unit 6 asks you to examine what teaching and learning really means to you and your teachers.

Contents

Unit 1 Understanding academic culture p2

- understand key terminology and concepts relating to academic culture

Unit 2 The transition to higher education p6

- identify common challenges for students in the early stages of higher education
- offer useful advice to students

Unit 3 Expectations of higher education institutions p10

- be more aware of expectations about teaching and learning in higher education institutions

Unit 4 Cross-cultural communication p13

- be more aware of reciprocal speech styles common in English-language academic contexts
- be better able to participate in academic situations, such as seminars

Unit 5 Time management p18

- identify factors involved in good time management
- analyse your own time-management skills and learn how to improve them

Unit 6 Philosophy of teaching and learning p22

- what constitutes good teaching
- what is involved in learning a subject

Web work p24

Extension activities p25

Glossary p26

Understanding academic culture

At the end of this unit, you will be able to:

- understand key terminology and concepts relating to academic culture

Task 1 Defining academic culture

When we go overseas to live and work, we have to get used to the new culture we have entered. For example:

> Seeing people eat with their hands may surprise you.

If you are a student, you will also have to get used to the academic culture of the institution in which you are studying.

1.1 Read and complete this definition of academic culture using some of the words in the box. Compare your completed definition with a partner's.

attitudes	~~beliefs~~	culture	regulations	research
rules	philosophy	study	thinking	values

Academic culture refers to the [a] *beliefs*, values and [b] _____ that exist in higher education institutions, particularly universities. Such a [c] _____ exists alongside the culture of the rest of the country. Academic culture includes, among other things, the rules and [d] _____ for appropriate behaviour on the part of teacher and student, and the [e] _____ that underlies teaching and learning at this level. It is also about the beliefs held by those working within such an institution, such as belief in original [f] _____ and critical [g] _____.

1.2 Use the words in the box to discuss the differences between the learning culture where you were previously with that of the institution you are currently attending.

Task 2 Important words in academic culture

2.1   What do you think is happening in the three photographs?

a

b

c

2.2   Match the terms (a–i) with the definitions (1–9). Check your answers with other students.

a.   Further education

b.   Undergraduate

c.   Personal tutor

d.   Lecturer

e.   Seminar

f.   Core course

g.   Social Sciences

h.   Plagiarism

i.   Formative assessment

1.   A student-focused class with two-way dialogue involving students.

2.   The person who plans and delivers a course to students.

3.   The use of other people's ideas or research without appropriate acknowledgment.

4.   An academic staff member assigned to students for support and guidance.

5.   Coursework that provides feedback and helps students do well in summatively assessed coursework and exams at a later date; it is not a given grade.

6.   Courses of study or training, usually not at university, that some people take after they have left secondary school.

7.   A compulsory course essential to your degree.

8.   The study of people in society, which includes Politics, Economics, Law, etc.

9.   The first level of study after leaving school, usually lasting three or four years.

1

2.3   Complete the sentences with the correct word from the pair of words supplied.

a.   ~~lecture~~ / seminar

The lecture was very crowded, so it was difficult to hear everything.

b.   lecturer / teaching assistant

Xavier stayed on at university after finishing his MA and worked as a _____ while studying for a PhD.

c.   research / plagiarism

It is tempting to copy things straight from the Web, but _____ is absolutely forbidden.

d.   tutor / personal tutor

If you have a problem with choosing your modules, you should make an appointment to discuss it with your _____.

e.   formative assessment / summative assessment

This course uses _____. The grades will count towards your final degree.

f.   higher education / further education

My mother left school at 16 without many qualifications, but she went back into _____ in her 20s to do a Photography course.

g.   core course / optional course

Jens has decided to take a(n) _____ in Spanish as well as his other subjects. He doesn't need the extra credits, but he wants to go to Spain in the summer.

h.   Humanities / Social Sciences

Anna is a _____ graduate. She has a degree in English and Drama.

i.   undergraduate / postgraduate

Leon worked in Australia for a year after he finished his first degree. Now he has gone back to university to study a(n) _____ course.

2.4 You have now worked with the following nine pairs of words. Discuss with a partner or in small groups the differences between them.

a. *lecture / seminar*

b. *lecturer / teaching assistant*

c. *research / plagiarism*

d. *tutor / personal tutor*

e. *formative assessment / summative assessment*

f. *higher education / further education*

g. *core course / optional course*

h. *Humanities / Social Sciences*

i. *undergraduate / postgraduate*

Reflect

Write a short essay comparing and contrasting the higher education academic culture in your country and the UK.

2 The transition to higher education

At the end of this unit, you will be able to:
- identify common challenges for students in the early stages of higher education
- offer useful advice to students

Task 1 Identifying challenges

1.1 These photographs show the challenges students face at university for the first time. What are they? Discuss in small groups.

1.2 Read the ten challenges and mark a cross on each line to show how you rate them. Add any other challenges you can think of:

a. making new friends

| not challenging | 1 | 2 | 3 | 4 | 5 | very challenging |

b. becoming a more independent learner

| not challenging | 1 | 2 | 3 | 4 | 5 | very challenging |

c. organising one's own time

| not challenging | 1 | 2 | 3 | 4 | 5 | very challenging |

d. doing research and writing original essays/reports

| not challenging | 1 | 2 | 3 | 4 | 5 | very challenging |

e. participating in seminars and tutorials

| not challenging | 1 | 2 | 3 | 4 | 5 | very challenging |

f.   attending lectures and taking notes

not challenging	1	2	3	4	5	very challenging

g.   sitting three-hour exams

not challenging	1	2	3	4	5	very challenging

h.   participating in teamwork activities

not challenging	1	2	3	4	5	very challenging

i.   adapting to the different expectations of teaching staff

not challenging	1	2	3	4	5	very challenging

j.   looking after yourself

not challenging	1	2	3	4	5	very challenging

•   _____

not challenging	1	2	3	4	5	very challenging

•   _____

not challenging	1	2	3	4	5	very challenging

1.3   **Discuss your ratings with a partner, giving reasons for your choices. Explain your five most and five least challenging things to the class.**

Task 2 Offering advice

2.1 Read the comments made by four undergraduates after their first term at university. Which ones are similar to your own experiences? Write something about yourself at the end.

a

'I did not organise the time very well, and this led to not finishing my written assignment.'

b

'Like all overseas students – I need to find ways of increasing my vocabulary.'

c

'The reason for my poor performance is that I haven't put in enough effort. I think many of us have had similar problems because we were not sure what the tutors expected from us and what the module required.'

d

'I felt really nervous the first time I had to participate in a seminar. Even though I wanted to contribute, I couldn't find the right words. And some of the other students talked so much and so quickly that I found it difficult to interrupt.'

e

_____

_____

_____

2.2 Work with a partner to discuss the best advice you could give the students. Present your advice to the class and note down any advice you had not discussed.

Task 3 Asking for help

3.1   Your personal tutor is there to help you with any issue you may be experiencing, whether academic or of a personal nature.

Work with a partner to brainstorm three issues you are facing or think you might face. How would you discuss these with your personal tutor?

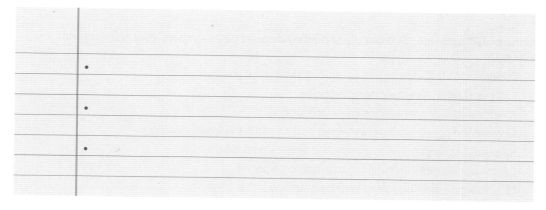

3.2   Role-play with your partner the conversation between you and your personal tutor.

Reflect

Write a letter to a friend who is still at school describing three differences between school and university life and give your friend some advice about what to expect.

Expectations of higher education institutions

At the end of this unit, you will:

- be more aware of expectations about teaching and learning in higher education institutions

Task 1 General expectations

The expectations when you start your course of study may affect the outcome. You may be pleasantly surprised by some aspects and disappointed or shocked by others. Being prepared will help avoid any unnecessary surprises!

1.1 **Are the statements true (T), false (F) or do they depend (D)? Compare your answers with a partner.**

a.   Lectures are likely to have 100 or more students in attendance.   ☐

b.   Examinations are normally multiple-choice.   ☐

c.   A mark of 60% or over is considered very good.   ☐

d.   Libraries are poorly stocked, with most books held in the reserve section.   ☐

e.   Students are very serious and have little time for relaxation.   ☐

f.   Coursework is more important than examined work.   ☐

g.   Most students are living away from their families.   ☐

h.   Staff address students by their family names.   ☐

i.   Attendance at lectures is compulsory.   ☐

j.   A first-class degree is hard to obtain.   ☐

1.2 **Which of the true statements surprise/shock you?**

Task 2 Expectations of lecturers

2.1 **Decide what you think the main duties of a lecturer are. Discuss your ideas with a partner.**

2.2 **Discuss and decide which of the following you would expect of a lecturer in a higher education institution. Why/Why not? Compare your choices with other students.**

I would expect a lecturer to …

a.   give interesting lectures.   ☐

b.   supply handouts about the lecture before or afterwards.   ☐

c.   be available at any time to answer queries.   ☐

d.   check assignments for language errors before submission.   ☐

e.   set and mark assignments.   ☐

f.   organise social events for the class.   ☐

g.   know students' first names and use them.   ☐

h.   be known by his/her first name.   ☐

i.   help students to find jobs after graduation.   ☐

j.   be flexible about submission deadlines.   ☐

Task 3 Expectations of students

3.1 Read the statements describing what lecturers may expect from students in a higher education institution. Discuss with a partner which column of the table you would put the statements in and why. Add anything else you can think of.

a. Attend all lectures, seminars and tutorials punctually.

b. Let the lecturer know if they are going to be absent.

c. Take notes from the lecture.

d. Read around the subject matter of the lecture.

e. Participate in seminar discussions and answer questions.

f. Give presentations.

g. Use the library for research.

h. Participate in group and teamwork activities.

i. Help the lecturer by cleaning the board or carrying books.

j. Speak to the lecturer if they have a personal problem.

k. Join a university club or society.

l. Get a part-time job to help with finances.

m. Buy small presents at the end of the term/semester to thank the lecturer.

- _____
- _____
- _____

students are expected to ...	students aren't expected to ...

3

Task 4 Critical incidents

4.1 Discuss the following four situations which might occur when you are studying. Choose the
most appropriate solution from the choices (1–4). Justify your ideas with reference to your
own experience. Note that more than one answer may be acceptable in each case.

a. You are 20 minutes late for a lecture. When you arrive, you can see from the door that the
lecture has already started. What would be the best thing to do?

1. Go in, walk up to the lecturer and apologise.

2. Wait outside until the lecture is over and then apologise to the lecturer.

3. Knock and wait to be told to enter.

4. Enter quietly and take a seat, trying not to be noticed.

Note: *Do you think class size makes a difference?*

b. You are given some coursework to complete in two days' time. This is very difficult for you
because your parents have just come to visit and expect you to show them around. What is
the best solution?

1. Explain the situation to your tutor and ask for an extension.

2. Be absent from class when you have to hand the coursework in.

3. Go to class without the coursework and say nothing.

4. Tell your parents they will have to entertain themselves.

c. You need to ask for an extension to your coursework submission date because you have
not finished an important essay for another subject. What would you be most likely to do?

1. Say you were sick and have a medical certificate.

2. Say you had problems with your laptop and lost your work.

3. Say you had too many assignments due in at the same time.

4. Say you had relations visiting you.

d. Your personal tutor has asked to see you urgently and has suggested it is about a disciplinary
matter. Which of these options is most likely to be the problem?

1. You haven't returned a library book due a week before.

2. You lent your lecture notes to a friend who was absent.

3. You handed in an identical essay to a friend, as you were told to work together.

4. You broke a test tube in the Chemistry laboratory.

Reflect

Hold a mini class debate on the proposition: *'Everyone should go to university.'*

4 Cross-cultural communication

At the end of this unit, you will:

- be more aware of reciprocal speech styles common in English-language academic contexts
- be better able to participate in academic situations, such as seminars

Task 1 Feeling at ease when you speak

You are judged in universities both by what you say and by what you write. When you write, you have more time to compose your thoughts, whereas participating in class discussions requires more rapid responses and can be stressful for both native and non-native speakers. As speaking can be stressful, it is worth thinking about how to put yourself at ease before speaking. An important aspect of this is to feel confident about conventions of speaking, especially in a different cultural environment.

1.1 **One source of uncertainty is the correct form of address. Which of the following titles have you used with academic staff you have worked with? Discuss with other students.**

   a.   first name, e.g., Mike ☐

   b.   academic title, e.g., teacher, doctor, professor ☐

   c.   academic title with surname, e.g., Dr Giddings ☐

   d.   family name, e.g., Mr, Mrs or Ms Fernandes ☐

   e.   madam or sir ☐

   f.   dear, mate, etc. ☐

   g.   other ☐

1.2 **Your lecturer is called Dr Meadows. Your class is a large one and it is the second week of term. You pass Dr Meadows in the corridor one day. How would you greet her?**

   a.   Good morning, doctor.

   b.   Good morning, Dr Meadows.

   c.   Good morning, madam.

   d.   Good morning, dear.

1.3 **Talk about your experiences and conclusions as a class and establish a few criteria for addressing staff.**

1.4 **Are the statements true (T) or false (F)? Discuss with a partner, giving reasons.**

   a.   The way you address someone in a hierarchical relationship (such as between teacher and student) should be negotiated by the person in the higher position. ☐

   b.   You should never address a lecturer by his or her first name. ☐

   c.   Academic staff may ask to be called by their first names, especially in smaller groups. ☐

   d.   You won't offend academic staff by addressing them incorrectly. They will understand if you make a mistake. ☐

   e.   You should ask someone how they would like to be addressed if you aren't sure. ☐

4

Task 2 Reciprocal speech style

Uncertainty about how to express your thoughts can also inhibit your contribution. In a seminar, you are expected to listen to the tutor and other members of the group, but also respond immediately (in words) to what they say. This style of exchange can be termed 'reciprocal speech style'.

2.1 **The following extract is a typical exchange that you might hear in a seminar. The exchange involves asking and answering questions and adding comments. Identify this pattern in the conversation below by matching the functions (a–c) to the appropriate phrase (1–3).**

    a.   Ask

    b.   Answer

    c.   Add

Student:		Do you think the recent climate changes can be attributed to global warming?
Tutor:	☐ 1.	No, I don't actually.
	☐ 2.	I think they are part of the normal pattern of climate change. If you look at recorded weather charts kept over the last 200 years, you'll see that, in 1857, there were extremely high temperatures in the UK.
	☐ 3.	What about you? Do you think global warming exists?
Student:		Well, …

Task 3 Applying discussion techniques

3.1 *Answer* the opinion-seeking questions.

    a.   Do you think capital punishment is acceptable?

    b.   Should we ban laboratory testing of cosmetics on animals?

    c.   Should university education be free?

    d.   Should all students be made to learn at least one foreign language?

    e.   Do you think young people spend too much time online?

3.2 *Add* comments to your answers above. Choose from this list:

    1.   The financial implications would be very heavy.

    2.   All life is sacred.

    3.   There are other ways to do this such as …

    4.   Communication with people from different nations is becoming more and more important.

    5.   More and more young people are suffering from eye strain.

3.3 *Ask* further questions on these topics. Choose from this list:

    i.   What did children used to do in their free time?

    ii.   Would that deter people from committing crimes?

    iii.   Isn't English a global language?

    iv.   Who would benefit?

    v.   What do you think about testing new medicines?

3.4 Choose one of the questions (a–e) from Task 3.1 and construct a discussion with another student using the *Answer-Add-Ask* statements above and continuing with your own ideas.

Task 4 Giving yourself thinking time

4.1 Match the techniques for buying yourself time (a–d) with the correct picture (1–4). Check your answers with a partner. In pairs, evaluate the techniques, trying to find an advantage and disadvantage for each one.

a.   Pretend you haven't heard.   ☐

b.   Repeat the question.   ☐

c.   Use delaying noises.   ☐

d.   Begin speaking by saying: 'It depends …'   ☐

1

?

'Sorry?'

2

What a tough question …

'What were the effects of the Industrial Revolution …?'

3

Where to begin?

'Umm, err, hmm …'

4

Here we go …

'It depends whether you are talking about short- or long-term effects.'

4.2 Think of other ways you can play for time. Write a list below and discuss your ideas with a partner.

Reflect

Explain the use of address terms in your country's schools and higher education institutions (100 words).

5 Time management

At the end of this unit you will be able to:

- identify factors involved in good time management
- analyse your own time-management skills and learn how to improve them

Time is something to be managed in British culture and good time-management skills are highly valued. How good are you at managing your time? This unit will find out.

Task 1 What is time management?

The first step towards using your time in higher education constructively is to clarify what is meant by good time management. It is then possible to decide what sort of activities contribute to your own effective management of time.

1.1 **Work with a partner to discuss which of the statements (a–g) best summarises what time management is and explain your reasons.**

Time management is …

a.   completing and submitting assignments as quickly as possible.

b.   knowing how to write an assignment the night before its deadline and still manage to attend classes the next day.

c.   developing a reliable system to organise and allocate time to tasks or situations so as to use the time effectively and achieve objectives.

d.   foregoing social activities in favour of study for up to one month before and during the examination period.

e.   learning how to use one's time more effectively to accomplish one's goals.

f.   maximising time available to you by studying until late in the evening.

g.   getting a friend or family member to remind you of deadlines and appointments.

1.2 **Decide which of the other statements give useful ideas for managing time and which statements need changing. Discuss your ideas with other students.**

Task 2 Importance of time management

It is useful to identify ways in which time management affects your life and the consequences of good and bad time management.

2.1 Think about which areas of your life as a student could be affected by good or bad time management and what the consequences of this could be. Complete the diagram with possible consequences. Add any other ideas you can think of.

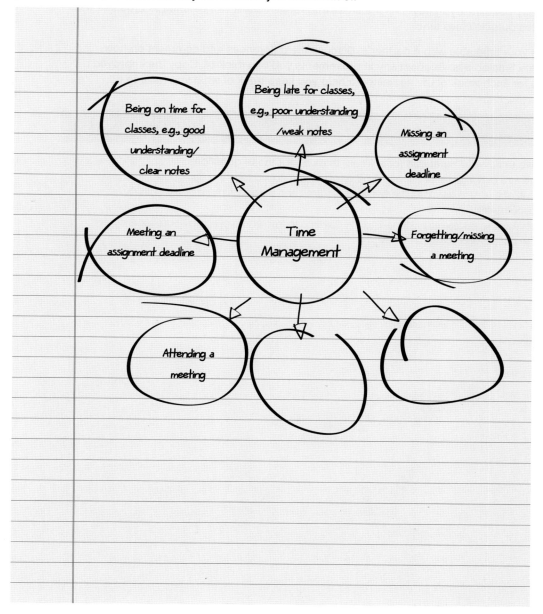

2.2 Compare your diagram with a partner's and discuss similarities and differences. Add any more ideas you have to your diagram.

Task 3 Improve your time management

Now that you have identified potential problem areas, you need to work on maximising effective time use. One strategy is to keep a record of how you organise your time. This raises your awareness of how long you spend on different activities and allows you to adjust and improve your time management.

3.1 Use the timetable on the opposite page to indicate when you are busy. Mark your class times and when you usually eat meals, sleep, do leisure activities, etc. Use a coloured circle to show any deadlines you have. All the times that remain blank can be used to organise your study times outside class time.

3.2 Compare your timetable with a partner's. Discuss the differences and comment on how realistic the timetable is. Suggest any improvements you can think of. Copy the improved timetable for each week of the semester to help you keep track of what you have to do.

Reflect

When you have used your timetable for a week, think about these questions:
- How well are you making use of the free time on your timetable during the day?
- Can you think of a way to use the time between lectures and seminars more constructively? How could you do this?
- Can you move some private study time into the daytime to free some evening hours for leisure activity? How could you do this?

	Monday	Tuesday	Wednesday	Thursday	Friday
06:00					
07:00					
08:00					
09:00					
10:00					
11:00					
12:00					
13:00					
14:00					
15:00					
16:00					
17:00					
18:00					
19:00					
20:00					
21:00					
22:00					
23:00					
24:00					

Philosophy of teaching and learning

At the end of this unit, you will be more aware of:

* what constitutes good teaching
* what is involved in learning a subject

Task 1 A good teacher?

1.1 Discuss the different teachers in the photographs. What kind of teacher would you like to have, and why?

1.2 Read the following list of features that you think should be found in a good teacher. Rank them from 1 to 10 (1 = the most important, 10 = the least important), giving reasons for your choices.

A good teacher …

a. explains clearly.

b. takes responsibility for a student passing or failing a course.

c. knows his/her subject very well and is able to answer any questions students may ask.

d. does not make mistakes.

e. is neat, well-groomed and smart in appearance.

f. has a clean and tidy office.

g. gives regular tests to check students' understanding.

h. sets exams only on what has been taught in class.

i. makes learning fun.

j. encourages learners to be independent and take risks.

Task 2 The good student

2.1 Discuss the different students in the photographs. What are they doing that is good for study?

2.2 Work with a partner. Read the list of features that you think should be found in a good student. Rank them in order of importance from 1 to 12 (1 = the most important, 12 = the least important), giving reasons for your choices.

A good student …

a. knows the answers to a teacher's questions. ☐

b. enters into discussion with the teacher if he/she disagrees. ☐

c. is willing to answer in class. ☐

d. is cheerful and popular. ☐

e. previews and reviews lectures. ☐

f. goes beyond the textbook in the pursuit of knowledge. ☐

g. is able to assess the quality of his/her own work. ☐

h. helps other class members. ☐

i. gets high marks. ☐

j. is able to think critically and creatively. ☐

k. is modest. ☐

l. knows when to work and when to play. ☐

Reflect

Describe a lecturer or teacher you respect and explain why.

Web work

Website 1

Different pond, different fish

http://www.ialf.edu/dpdf/march04page2.html

Review

This website gives access to various issues of a newsletter called *Different pond, different fish* written by Indonesian students. This is a fun, informative website with cartoons illustrating some of the points being made.

Task

Browse the site and share what you found interesting with your classmates.

Website 2

University of Twente, Holland: Academic Culture

http://www.utwente.nl/internationalstudents/preparing/files/utacademicculture/

Review

This website attempts to explain to international students the academic culture of the University of Twente and how it might be different from the culture in the student's country or a student's secondary school.

Task

Read the section entitled *Interaction in class* and watch the video on *Classroom interaction*. Write one or two paragraphs describing the similarities and differences between expected classroom interaction at the University of Twente and in your home country or secondary school.

Extension activities

Activity 1

Create a cartoon like the one from Website 1 in the web work activities. In your cartoon, highlight a misunderstanding that may occur due to differing expectations of higher education.

Activity 2

'According to the University of Twente, your best teachers are often your fellow students.' Debate this issue in class.

G

Glossary

academic conventions (n) Widely used and accepted practices that are agreed on at academic institutions. For example, standard practices in research, academic writing, attendance regulations, etc.

academic culture (n) The values and beliefs that exist in academic institutions, particularly those which inform and influence academic conventions.

analyse (v) To break an issue down into parts in order to study, identify and discuss their meaning and/or relevance.

assignment (n) A piece of work, generally written, that is set as part of an academic course and is normally completed out of class and submitted by a set date to be assessed.

belief (n) Something that is accepted to be right, often by a collection of people, even if it has not been (or cannot be) demonstrated as true. For example, many vegetarians hold the belief that killing animals is wrong.

core course (n) A course that must be completed as part of a programme in order to gain a qualification, such as a degree.

coursework (n) Work that is done as part of a course and that is normally assessed to form part of a student's final grade.

critical incident (n) A problematic or challenging event that may not appear to have an impact at the time, but subsequently has a critical outcome, i.e., an outcome that is insightful and/ or changes the views or behaviour of those it affects.

deadline (n) The date or time that something needs to be completed by. In academic situations, deadlines are normally given for handing in essays and assignments.

essay (n) An analytical piece of academic writing. Students are required to write essays as assignments and in exams so that their learning can be assessed.

evaluate (v) To assess information in terms of quality, relevance, objectivity and accuracy.

feedback (n) A response to an activity, process or product that gives information about how successful it was and deals with any problems that arose.

((v) = **feed back**)

first-class degree (n) The highest classification of a bachelor degree that an undergraduate can achieve at a British college or university. Students generally receive a first-class degree (a first) if they score high overall marks (of 70% or over) in exams and/or coursework.

formative assessment (n) Tests or unassessed coursework that does not count towards a final grade, but instead provides feedback and help for students in preparation for assessed coursework and exams at a later date.

further education (n) Post-compulsory education at pre-degree level. For example, at a vocational, technical or art college or institute. It may offer students the chance to take qualifications also available at the level of compulsory schooling and/or tertiary and degree courses.

goal (n) An aim or end purpose that someone tries to achieve or reach.

handout (n) Paper-based information that is given out by the lecturer or speaker in a lecture, seminar or tutorial. It usually gives a summary, bibliography or extra information connected with the lecture topic. It may also be a worksheet.

higher education (n) Tertiary education that is beyond the level of secondary education and that usually offers first and higher degrees. A university is an institution of higher education.

Humanities (n) Arts subjects that are concerned with human thought and culture, sometimes known as the Liberal Arts, such as: Philosophy, Literature, Languages and History of Art. These departments are normally grouped together to form a faculty in a university.

independent learning (n) This is where learners take responsibility for their own learning, and are able to develop their personal learning styles. It allows learners to make decisions and set goals that meet their own needs.

key concepts (n) Important ideas and beliefs. For example, in modern British academic culture, independent learning is a key concept.

key terminology (n) The most important information given, such as the main points in a lecture, essay or set of instructions.

learning style (n) A style of thinking about, processing and remembering information that you have to learn. Different styles can be classified in a variety of ways. For example, you may have an analytical learning style.

lecture (n) A formal talk or presentation given to inform or instruct people. In tertiary education, lectures are usually delivered by academic staff to large groups of students.

multiple-choice (adj) A question or task where students are given a set of several possible answers, normally only one of which is correct. They are required to choose the correct answer.

objective (adj) (n) 1 (adj) Not influenced by personal feelings or emotions. 2 (n) The aim, or what you want to achieve from an activity.

optional course (n) A course that is not compulsory for the completion of a degree. Students may be asked to supplement their core courses by choosing one or more optional courses.

participate (v) To get involved or take part in something. For example, it is important to participate actively in seminars.

personal tutor (n) A tutor who is assigned to a group of students to provide advice, guidance and support on personal and study matters within their experience and expertise.

philosophy (n) A system of values or set of beliefs that affect how someone lives his/her life.

plagiarism (n) Presenting someone else's work, i.e., written text, data, images, recording, as your own. This includes:

• copying or paraphrasing material from any source without a citation;

• presenting other people's ideas without a citation;

• working with others and then presenting the work as if it was completed independently.

Plagiarism is not always deliberate, and it is important to adopt the academic conventions of always indicating ideas and work that are not your own, and referencing all your sources correctly.

postgraduate (n) (adj) 1 (n) A student who has completed a university degree and is studying a higher-level course at post-first degree level. 2 (adj) Used to describe such a student or his/her studies.

presentation (n) A short lecture, talk or demonstration given in front of an audience. The speaker prepares his or her presentation in advance and will often use visual aids or realia to illustrate it.

reciprocal speech style (n) A description of the speech style where the listener is required to respond immediately to the speaker using a similar style. This is expected in situations such as seminars where, for example, a student may respond to a speaker's comments, add information and pose questions.

reference (n) (v) 1 (n) Acknowledgment of the sources of ideas and information that you use in written work and oral presentations. 2 (v) To acknowledge or mention the sources of information.

research (n) (v) 1 (n) Information collected from a variety of sources about a specific topic. 2 (v) To gather information from a variety of sources and analyse and compare it.

secondary education (n) Compulsory education between the ages of 11/12 and 16 at a secondary school.

seminar (n) A small group discussion led by a tutor, lecturer or guest speaker. Students are expected to take an active part in a seminar.

Social Sciences (n) Science subjects that are connected with the study of people in society, including Politics, Economics, History, Anthropology, Law, etc. These departments are normally grouped together to form a faculty in a university.

strategy (n) A plan of action that you follow when you want to achieve a particular goal. For example, it is possible to have a clear strategy for passing an exam.

teamwork (n) Working supportively and cooperatively in a group to achieve a common goal.

technique (n) A method or way of doing something that involves skill and/or efficiency. For example, it is possible to learn useful techniques for answering exam questions.

time management (n) The ability to organise your time so that you use it more effectively and efficiently.

tutorial (n) A small group discussion or one-to-one meeting with a tutor.

Notes

Notes

Notes

Notes

Published by
Garnet Publishing Ltd
8 Southern Court
South Street
Reading RG1 4QS, UK

This book is based on an original concept devised by
Dr Anthony Manning and Mrs Frances Russell.

ISBN 978 1 78260 176 0

British Library Cataloguing-in-Publication Data
A catalogue record for this book is available from the British
Library.

Production

Project Manager:	Clare Chandler
Editorial team:	Clare Chandler, Sophia Hopton, Martin Moore
Design & Layout:	Madeleine Maddock
Photography:	iStockphoto, Shutterstock

Garnet Publishing and the authors of TASK would like to
thank the staff and students of the International Foundation
Programme at the University of Reading for their respective
roles in the development of these teaching materials.

Garnet Publishing would like to thank Lucy Norris and Fiona
McGarry for their contribution to the First edition of the
TASK series.

All website URLs provided in this publication were correct at
the time of printing. If any URL does not work, please contact
your tutor, who will help you find similar resources.

Printed and bound in Lebanon by International Press:
interpress@int-press.com